PAINTING FREE
Lines, Colors, and Shapes

PAINTING FREE
LINES, COLORS, AND SHAPES

by MICKEY KLAR MARKS

paintings by Edith Alberts
photographs by David Rosenfeld

The Dial Press   New York   1965

FOR

NAT and ISEE

W<small>E LIVE IN THE SPACE AGE AND ABSTRACT PAINTING,</small> like all art through the centuries, reflects the time.

An abstract is shapes on space. Triangles, squares and rounded forms are arranged to please, provoke or excite the eye. An abstract reaches for the places we are yet to visit, things we are yet to experience.

The aim of this book is to make you reach: make you see with your own eyes not only what exists around you, but also what you imagine might or could exist. It is not an "art book" and will give no lessons in perspective or academic painting. It is a primer, an elementary study which will put materials into your hands so that you can turn out some very decorative and perhaps some very good paintings of your own. Its purpose is to encourage your own pictorial imagination.

Don't be disappointed if you do not reproduce exactly any of the works shown at the end of the book. Your paintings will not, and are not intended to, be copies. The illustrations serve only as examples of the various techniques which you, as the artist, will develop into something of your own.

Sometime in your life you must have played "let's pretend." Let's pretend "I'm the daddy and you're the mommy." Or, when you were older, you daydreamed that you were a famous actress or the President of the United States or a second Willie Mays. You gave your imagination free rein.

Instead of thinking those daydreams, you can paint them.

Each person's eyes alone translate the images around him, and this personal image influences his reaction to people, places and things, and assuredly to painting.

If Father painted a portrait of Aunt Jane, for example, he might picture her as serene as a queen. You might very well see Aunt Jane as someone from outer space and immortalize her on canvas as having a green square for a face and no eyes, because an abstract painting is a composition suggested by an object or figure. That suggestion is turned into a design which, with the use of line, color and texture, recalls the original object or figure.

For instance when is a tree not a tree? Never! It is always

a tree, but a maple seen by Father and the same maple seen by you are trees of different colors.

Abstract painting is not only individual but inventive. To quote Wassily Kandinsky, who is referred to as the father of this form of painting: "Everything is permitted."

The techniques are limitless. You can scumble, butter, glaze, drip, dribble, brush, spray, spatter and much more. Don't the above words make you itch to pick up a brush and get started? Patience: another word or two and you can begin to paint, and terms such as scumble and butter will be explained as each example is presented.

Paints range from hardware-store enamels to oils; brushes include anything from a camel's-hair painting brush to an old hairbrush.

The following pages will give you step by step instructions for several paintings in order to acquaint you with some techniques and materials.

Half the fun of painting is to experiment. Play with colors; get varied tones by adding a little more of this and a little less of that. Try different compositions and unusual arrangements until you come up with something that pleases you. This book is a jumping-off place; the launching pad from which your own pictorial rocket blasts off.

Before you start the first painting, however, it will help if you understand the make-up of an abstract.

Here is a still-life arrangement: a straw hat, a ukulele, a

sea fan and a piece of driftwood set against a burlap
drapery.

In the painting pictured opposite, the artist has reduced
the real objects to a design. The ukulele is a curved line,
the hat a half circle, the sea fan a black oblong set against
the drapery, which is now a light form. The free form at
the bottom of the canvas was once the driftwood.

The painting remains a still-life arrangement, but it has
been transformed into shapes and graded tones. To quote

Mondrian: "The surface of things gives enjoyment, their inwardness gives life."

Now turn the book all ways. You will find that the painting is attractive no matter how you look at it, for a good abstract should hold together even if you look at it standing on your head.

You can see that although abstract painting may appear to be slapdash, it isn't so. A basic idea or concept should be thought out before you start to paint anything.

In mixing your colors, use dark oil paints sparingly. Too much black or burnt sienna will give you a muddy result. Draw a balanced design so that the eye is focused on the canvas. Shapes that sweep, strong lines and dynamic colors will reward you with an interesting composition.

Few materials will be needed for the paintings shown here so don't rush out and buy yourself a complete artist's kit from easel to smock. You will need the following: seven tubes of oil paints (burnt sienna, cobalt blue, cadmium light yellow, cadmium light red, light green, black and white); or, if you prefer, one large black, one large white, and five small tubes of colors of your own choice; a half-inch painting brush; a fine brush; one can of black enamel paint; two cans of flat spray paint (one white, one black); a bottle of turpentine; one can of Demar varnish; a painting knife; masking tape; a rolling pin; an old hairbrush or a whisk broom; clear plastic sandwich paper; gesso; glue-all; a roll of string; sand; and some rags.

You can paint on anything from stretched canvas to

12

paper, but the backgrounds suggested are wallboard (masonite), canvas board or plywood. Both masonite and plywood can be bought at any lumberyard and cut to size, and they are inexpensive. Canvas board can be found in all art stores and many department stores.

A piece of tin foil can serve as a palette, and an empty jar or a clean tin can can be used to mix paints and turpentine instead of a painting cup.

Since the brushes can be used over and over again, buy good ones because they last much longer. To keep brushes clean, dip them into turpentine, wipe with a cloth and then wash them in soap and water. If any paint sticks to you (and it is almost certain that some will) turpentine first and then a good wash with soap and water will clean it off.

Work on a clean table or working surface and have a rag handy and your materials ready before you start to paint.

SEA CAVE

MATERIALS

Masonite (rough side), rolling pin, clear plastic paper, flat black spray paint, white, blue and green oil paints, half-inch painting brush, turpentine.

Step 1

Prepare your masonite board by spraying with flat black spray paint, leaving a portion in the center unsprayed. (The paint will dry in a few minutes.) Don't use an enamel spray paint because there will be too high a gloss. Flat paint sinks into the board or canvas and gives a good undercoat.

Step 2

Cut a piece of plastic paper a little larger than the board, and place it on the table. Squeeze green, blue and some stripes of white oil paint as if you were putting tooth-paste on a toothbrush.

Step 3

Wet your brush with turpentine and sprinkle some turpentine from it on paints and paper.

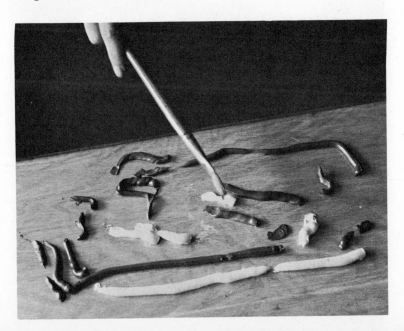

Step 4

Place the board over the paper. Then turn the board and paper over. The painted paper will stick to the board.

Step 5

Push the paints around with the rolling pin. Roll in all directions. Try to push the paints so that they will melt into the design you want.

16

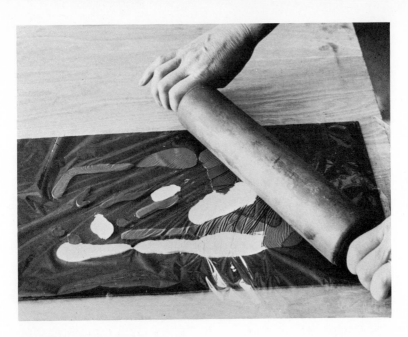

Step 6

If colors aren't spreading enough, lift up a corner of the plastic paper and sprinkle more turpentine on the dry areas.

Step 7

Lift off plastic paper and there is your abstract painting.

Let the painting dry overnight, then spray with Demar varnish.

Paintings sometimes take longer to dry if the weather is humid or if you have applied your paints thickly. Be sure your painting is bone dry before you varnish. All paintings should be sprayed with varnish to give them a gloss and make the colors spring to life as well as to preserve the work.

Designs are unlimited with the rolling pin method. You will never get the same result twice. There will always be some variation which makes this simple technique fascinating.

A picture of "Sea Cave" is at the end of this book.

DESERT SUNRISE

MATERIALS

Masonite (smooth side), black spray paint, stiff brush (hairbrush or whisk broom), painting knife, sand, black enamel, stick or pencil, black, burnt sienna, white and yellow oil paints.

Step 1

Prepare the board by spraying it with black spray paint. Let it dry.

Step 2

Squeeze a generous amount of burnt sienna and a small amount of white oil paint onto your palette or tin foil and mix together. Blend the paints thoroughly with the painting knife. Put a good glob of paint on the painting knife and butter the board thickly, exactly as you would butter a slice of bread.

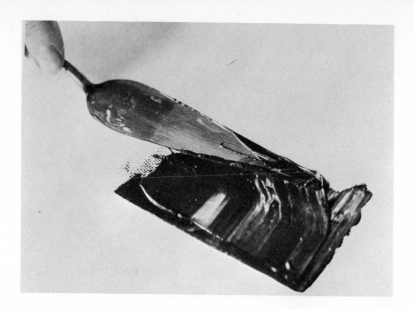

Step 3

Wipe the painting knife on a rag and mix a small amount of yellow and white oil paint together. Blend the colors thoroughly. Put some paint on your painting knife and butter the board again, more in the center and left of the board for highlights.

Step 4

While the painting is still wet, take a stiff brush and push the brush up and down the board. The background will take on a textured look.

Let the board dry overnight. Be sure the painting is bone dry before proceeding to the next step.

As we mentioned earlier, various conditions and elements may keep the board wet for a longer period. Generally speaking, however, your board should be ready for work the following day.

Step 5

Stir the contents of a can of black enamel paint with a stick. Tilt the board at an angle, and, using the stick, drip black enamel on the painting from the top of the board, so that the paint drips down it. Drip paint more heavily at the bottom of the board.

Step 6

Replace the board on the work table so that it lies flat. Take a handful of sand and scatter it all over the board.

22

The sand will stick to the enamel, which is still wet, but it will not adhere to the dry undercoat.

Step 7

Let the painting set for about fifteen minutes and then shake off excess sand. You will see that the sand has stuck only to the drippings.

Step 8

Wait half an hour and then add a few highlights. Paint around some of the sand drippings using a fine brush and yellow oil paint. If your yellow paint is too dry, add a little turpentine to thin it.

Step 9

After the painting is dry, spray the entire board with Demar varnish.

You can see the finished "Desert Sunrise" at the back of this book.

ELEMENTS

MATERIALS

Masonite (smooth side), white spray paint, black spray paint, half-inch painting brush, turpentine, glue-all, black enamel paint, roll of string, red and white oil paints.

Step 1

Prepare the board by spraying it with white spray paint.

Step 2

Unroll the string on the board at random.

Step 3

Spray the left-hand side of the board with a mist of black spray paint. Spray more heavily on the bottom of the board. Spray over the string.

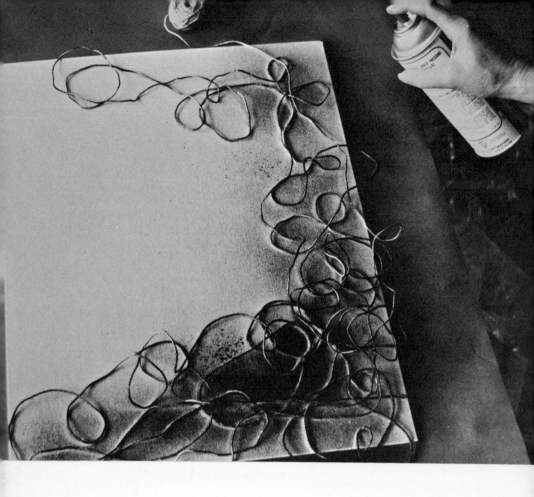

Step 4

Drip glue-all in a free-form design on the top ⬩
of the board. Spot a few squiggles of glue-all on th
of the board. Do *not* move the board until the glue-a
hardened and dried. This will take about three or
hours.

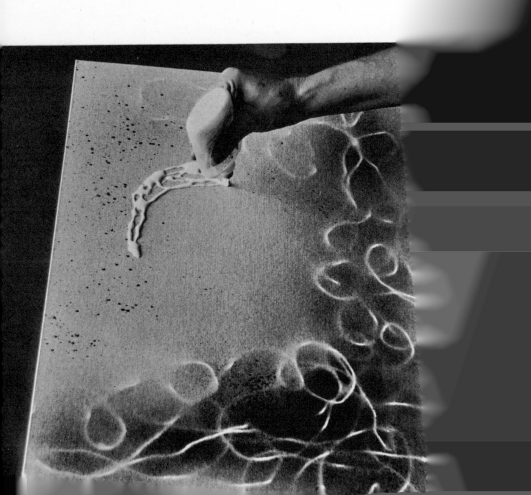

Step 5

Make a glaze by mixing a small amount of red paint with a few drops of turpentine. Apply the glaze with a half-inch painting brush to the free-form blobs of hardened glue-all. The glaze will brush on smoothly.

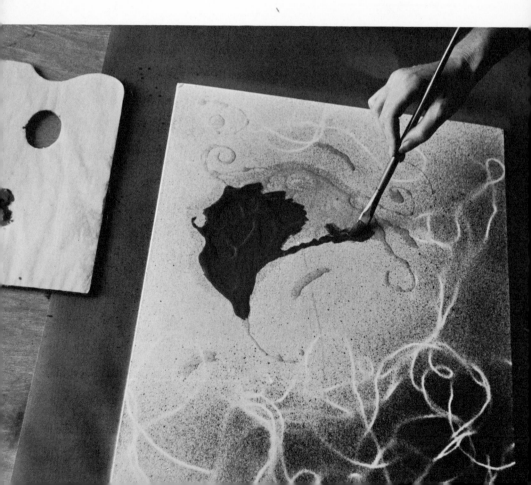

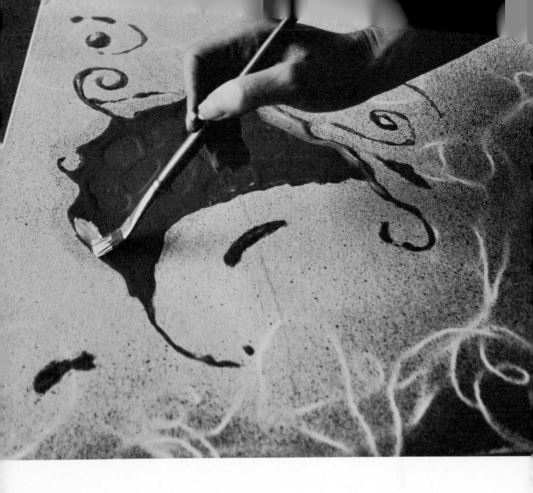

Step 6

Highlight the free-form area with touches of white oil paint using the half-inch painting brush.

Step 7

Dribble black enamel paint with a stick or pencil, or the handle of the paint brush following the shapes of the white lines. Dribble black enamel to outer edge of glazed free-form area.

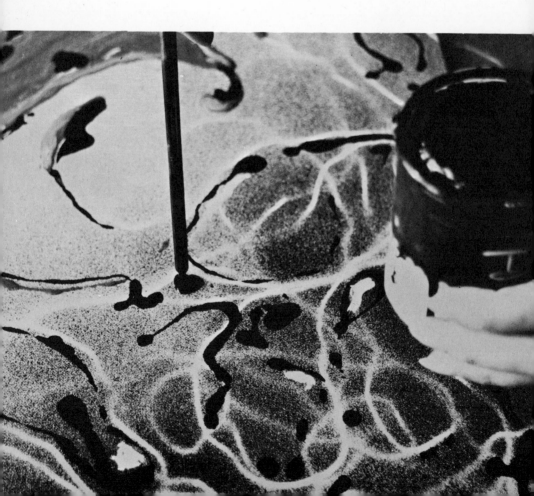

Step 8

Put a coat of varnish on the painting when it is dry.

A color photograph of "Elements" is in the picture section at the end of this book.

CORRIDORS

MATERIALS

Piece of plywood (try to pick a piece with a good grain in it), fine brush, half-inch painting brush, ruler, pencil, turpentine, black, white, burnt sienna and yellow oil paints.

Step 1

Make a wash with burnt sienna and turpentine. A wash is a water-like mixture made of lots of turpentine and a small amount of paint. Using your half-inch brush, start at the top of the board and paint evenly, covering the entire board.

Step 2

Let the wash dry, which will take approximately ten minutes. Wood absorbs paint quickly, and the grain will show through.

Step 3

Draw five squares, one within the other, using the pencil and ruler.

Step 4

Paint the center square solid white. Paint a yellow circle in the center of the white square. Use the fine brush.

Step 5

Paint the next square burnt sienna.

Step 6

Do not paint the third square.

Step 7

Paint the fourth square black.

Step 8

Do not paint the last square. Let the painting dry for half an hour.

Step 9

Take black oil paint, and using the ruler and the fine brush, outline the last square with black paint. Wipe your ruler each time you remove it from the board. If paint seems too thick, add a little turpentine to it so that the brush will move easily.

Step 10

Using the ruler and black oil paint draw a line from the corner of the white square to the outer edge of the last square.

Step 11

Starting at the same point, draw a second line letting it widen as it gets to the outer square. Fill in with black paint. Repeat at the other three corners.

Step 12

Mix white oil paint with a drop of black to get gray. Paint the top and bottom of the third square in gray. Paint left and right side of last square in gray. Varnish the entire painting when it is dry.

A photograph of "Corridors" is in the picture section.

STUDY IN BLOCKS

MATERIALS

Canvas board, half-inch painting brush, fine brush, painting knife, sand, ruler, masking tape, pencil, turpentine, yellow, burnt sienna, black, white, green, red and blue oil paints.

Step 1

Draw a composition of rectangles with the ruler and pencil.

Step 2

Blend white, a little burnt sienna and a small amount of turpentine together. Mix well. Paint the entire background of the canvas board using the half-inch painting brush.

Step 3

Clean your brushes before changing colors. Mix burnt sienna with a little turpentine. Paint the center bottom rectangle.

Step 4

Mix green with a little blue and paint top rectangle.

Step 5

Start at left-hand side of bottom rectangle and paint with clear black. Gradually add white to the black and lighten from the center to the right. This will give a shadowed effect.

Step 6

Paint the top right rectangle clear black.

Step 7

Paint the center rectangle red. Let the painting dry thoroughly.

Step 8

Mix a blue and green wash. Use a lot of turpentine to get a watery mixture. Wash the entire background (do not use wash on the blocks) then gently wipe off with a clean cloth. The wash will dry in approximately ten minutes.

Step 9

Place masking tape around the outside edges of the two unpainted rectangles.

Step 10

Mix yellow oil paint with a tablespoonful of sand. Be sure to blend thoroughly. Add a little turpentine if the mixture seems too dry to apply easily. Using the painting knife, butter the two rectangles that have been masked off with a large amount of sanded paint. Build up the thickness of these rectangles by adding more sand and paint.

Step 11

Carefully remove masking tape. Let the painting dry for a few days.

Step 12

Mix burnt sienna and black oil paint together. Paint thickly over the burnt sienna rectangle. Scratch wet paint across and then down with the handle of your brush.

Step 13

Squeeze a small amount of white oil paint onto your palette or tin foil and, with the painting knife, scumble over the green rectangle.

Scumbling means using the edge of the painting knife touched with a bit of paint, and lightly pulling it across the canvas or area you wish to cover partially. In scumbling, the color beneath shows through.

Step 14

With the fine brush, draw a black line around the outside edges of the green and the large yellow rectangles. Put a few green dots at random on the canvas with the tip of the fine brush.

See the back of the book for a picture of the finished "Study in Blocks."

BRIGHT LIGHTS

MATERIALS

Masonite (rough side), gesso, half-inch painting brush, rolling pin, clear plastic paper, painting knife, masking tape, turpentine, red, yellow, blue and green oil paints.

Step 1

Prepare board with gesso. Gesso is a chalklike plastery substance, like marshmallow topping, and makes a good base for any painting. It dries quickly, and the brush can be washed with water after usage. Paint the entire board with gesso. Give the board a second or third coat, allowing ten minutes in between each coat.

Step 2

Make a wash with blue oil paint and turpentine. Apply the wash to the right-hand corner of the board and let it drip down. Make a wash with a little green oil paint and turpentine, and while the blue wash is still wet, apply the green wash on just a corner of the blue and let the colors run together.

Step 3

Turn the board upside down and apply the blue wash, on what appears in the photograph to be the top right corner of the board. Let the wash run. Add a bit of green wash exactly as you did to the first wash. Hold the board in the same position for about five minutes until it is dry.

Step 4

Turn your board back to its original position. Dip the brush in the green wash and spatter upper left corner. Dip the brush into the blue wash and spatter in the same area. You can control the spatter by hitting the brush against your wrist as shown in the photograph. If you spatter wildly

your painting will look as if it had developed a bad case of the measles.

Step 5

Apply masking tape to areas as shown in the photograph below.

Step 6

Squeeze red, blue, green and yellow oil paint around the tape, directly from the tube onto the board.

Step 7

Sprinkle some drops of turpentine with a brush on the blobs of paint. Cover entire board with clear plastic paper and, with the rolling pin, push the paints around in different directions.

When you place the paper on the board, sometimes you may make a mistake and a speck of paint may move from the pattern or the paper may become wrinkled while you are rolling the paints. Nothing is lost, however, for these accidents often give an added interest to the finished work. Straighten out the paper and keep rolling.

Step 8

Peel off plastic paper. Remove masking tape.

Step 9

Crumple the plastic paper so you can hold the clean side. Then press the oil painted side onto the board in areas that need highlights.

Step 10

Put a small amount of blue oil paint on the painting knife and scumble over the red, in the center of the board. Add a few slashed lines in yellow, at the top of the same area. Pull a blue line at the bottom of the board with the painting knife.

Step 11

Since the use of the rolling pin probably will result in a design that is slightly different from the one shown here, use your imagination and enhance or strengthen your composition by breaking up large masses of color with highlights or lines.

Step 12

Allow the painting to dry. Spray it with Demar varnish.

A picture of "Bright Lights" is in the color section.

Now that you have had a taste of abstract painting you may want to go further in your art studies.

Go to museums and galleries and see the work of such outstanding painters as Delaunay, Kline, Mondrian, Picasso, Kandinsky and Pollock among others. You will see that each man's work is highly individual; from the stark black forms on bright white canvas by Kline, to the gorgeous explosions of color that look like fireworks on the Fourth of July, by Kandinsky. You will learn by looking and you will develop a trained eye.

If you are a serious artist, you won't depend on happy accidents to create a good painting. To really know your craft you need the basic foundations of drawing, anatomy and perspective. The true artist has studied for years. He knows how to paint every detail of an eyelash, a muscle, a leaf or a flower. Only after he has learned to paint what he actually sees is he privileged to paint with his mind's eye, if he wishes to. Because of the changing world, different ways of expression constantly burst forth. Abstract painting is only one of them, and it is a way that never ceases to develop as long as there are talented, inventive artists who have something to say.

You might very well be one of them.

GLOSSARY

Brushing   Pulling a stiff brush through wet paint already applied to the canvas or board.

Buttering   Applying paint as if buttering a slice of bread.

Dripping   Dripping paint from a pencil, pointed tool or stick end of a paintbrush.

Dribbling   Same as dripping.

Glazing   Giving a high gloss by using varnish or glue-all.

Masking   Covering areas inside given space.

Painting   Applying colors.

Pulling   Using the edge of the painting knife.

Sanding   Putting sand on parts of the canvas where paint is still wet.

Scratching   Using a pencil or stick end of a paintbrush for making a design.

Scumbling   Applying paint with the edge of the painting knife, usually over a dry coat of paint.

Spattering	Shaking thin mixture of paint and turpentine off the tip of a paintbrush.
Spraying	Painting by the use of commercial spray paints.
Varnishing	Glazing certain areas, or preserving a painting.
Wash	Paint thinned with turpentine to a watery mixture and applied evenly.

SEA CAVE

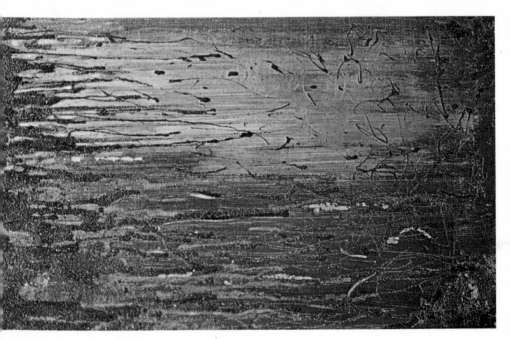

DESERT SUNRISE

CORRIDORS

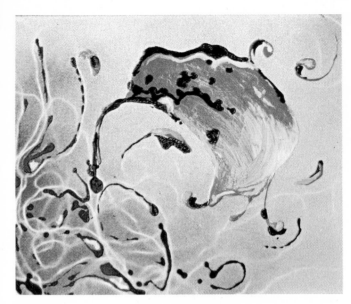

ELEMENTS

BRIGHT LIGHTS

STUDY IN BLOCKS